W9-CKI-384

FANCY FLOWERS

By NADIA HIGGINS

Illustrations by CHRIS BIGGIN

Music by DREW TEMPERANTE

CANTATA
LEARNING

WWW.CANTATALEARNING.COM

CANTATA
LEARNING

Published by Cantata Learning
1710 Roe Crest Drive
North Mankato, MN 56003
www.cantatalearning.com

A note to educators and librarians from the publisher: Cantata Learning has provided the following data to assist in book processing and suggested use of Cantata Learning product.

Publisher's Cataloging-in-Publication Data
Prepared by Librarian Consultant: Ann-Marie Begnaud
Library of Congress Control Number: 2016938073
 Fancy Flowers
 Series: My First Science Songs
 By Nadia Higgins
 Illustrations by Chris Biggin
 Music by Drew Temperante
 Summary: Learn how flowers help plants reproduce in this illustrated story set to music.
 ISBN: 978-1-63290-786-8 (library binding/CD)
Suggested Dewey and Subject Headings:
 Dewey: E 575.6
 LCSH Subject Headings: Flowers – Juvenile literature. | Flowers – Songs and music – Texts. | Flowers – Juvenile sound recordings.
 Sears Subject Headings: Flowers. | School songbooks. | Children's songs. | Popular music.
 BISAC Subject Headings: JUVENILE NONFICTION / Science & Nature / Flowers & Plants. | JUVENILE NONFICTION / Music / Songbooks. | JUVENILE NONFICTION / Science & Nature / Botany.

Book design and art direction: Tim Palin Creative
Editorial direction: Flat Sole Studio
Music direction: Elizabeth Draper
Music written and produced by Drew Temperante

Printed in the United States of America in North Mankato, Minnesota.
122016   0339CGS17

ACCESS THE MUSIC!
SCAN CODE WITH MOBILE APP
CANTATALEARNING.COM

TIPS TO SUPPORT LITERACY AT HOME

WHY READING AND SINGING WITH YOUR CHILD IS SO IMPORTANT

Daily reading with your child leads to increased academic achievement. Music and songs, specifically rhyming songs, are a fun and easy way to build early literacy and language development. Music skills correlate significantly with both phonological awareness and reading development. Singing helps build vocabulary and speech development. And reading and appreciating music together is a wonderful way to strengthen your relationship.

READ AND SING EVERY DAY!

TIPS FOR USING CANTATA LEARNING BOOKS AND SONGS DURING YOUR DAILY STORY TIME

1. As you sing and read, point out the different words on the page that rhyme. Suggest other words that rhyme.

2. Memorize simple rhymes such as Itsy Bitsy Spider and sing them together. This encourages comprehension skills and early literacy skills.

3. Use the questions in the back of each book to guide your singing and storytelling.

4. Read the included sheet music with your child while you listen to the song. How do the music notes correlate to the words of the song?

5. Sing along on the go and at home. Access music by scanning the QR code on each Cantata book, or by using the included CD. You can also stream or download the music for free to your computer, smartphone, or mobile device.

Devoting time to daily reading shows that you are available for your child. Together, you are building language, literacy, and listening skills.

Have fun reading and singing!

Flowers are fun to look at. They can smell nice, too. Some flowers even taste good. And did you know that plants need flowers to make seeds?

To learn more about fancy flowers, turn the page and sing along!

One, two, three, four, five, six!

Six plant parts and they go like this:
roots, stems, leaves,
flowers, fruit, and seeds!

fruit

seed

flower

leaf

Stem

root

Each part plays a special role.

Flowers help plants to grow and grow.

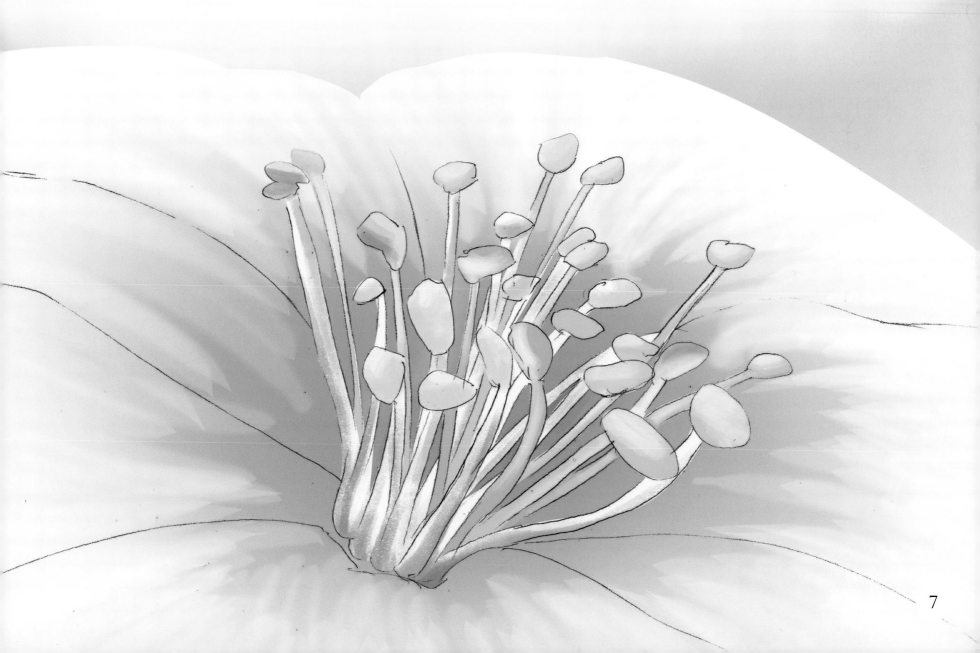

Flowers **attract** butterflies and bees,
which spread the **pollen** flowers need.

Then the flowers make fruit and seeds.
Oh, flowers, yes, they make seeds!

Flowers, they make quite a show
on a pond or a windy meadow.

Farmers grow flowers they hope to sell
in every color, shape, and smell.

11

Flowers attract butterflies and bees,
which spread the pollen flowers need.

Then the flowers make fruit and seeds.
Oh, flowers, yes, they make seeds!

Eat some flowers. Have a bowl of **cauliflower** casserole.

Butter **artichokes** and broccoli. Sip a cup of **chamomile** tea!

15

Everyone do the flower ballet,
swaying on a summer's day.

Open your petals. Shake them out,
so bees can see what you're all about.

Fill the air with a **scent** so sweet.
Butterflies will flutter at your feet.

Gather the pollen that they bring
for seeds to sprout new blooms next spring.

Flowers attract butterflies and bees,
which spread the pollen flowers need.

Then the flowers make fruit and seeds.
Oh, flowers, yes, they make seeds!

Life Cycle of a Plant

19

Flowers attract butterflies and bees,
which spread the pollen flowers need.

Then the flowers make fruit and seeds.
Oh, flowers, yes, they make seeds!

SONG LYRICS
Fancy Flowers

One, two, three, four, five, six!
Six plant parts and they go like this:
roots, stems, leaves,
flowers, fruit, and seeds!

Each part plays a special role.
Flowers help plants to grow and grow.

Flowers attract butterflies and bees,
which spread the pollen flowers need.
Then the flowers make fruit and seeds.
Oh, flowers, yes, they make seeds!

Flowers, they make quite a show
on a pond or a windy meadow.
Farmers grow flowers they hope to sell
in every color, shape, and smell.

Flowers attract butterflies and bees,
which spread the pollen flowers need.
Then the flowers make fruit and seeds.
Oh, flowers, yes, they make seeds!

Eat some flowers. Have a bowl
of cauliflower casserole.
Butter artichokes and broccoli.
Sip a cup of chamomile tea!

Everyone do the flower ballet,
swaying on a summer's day.
Open your petals. Shake them out,
so bees can see what you're all about.

Fill the air with a scent so sweet.
Butterflies will flutter at your feet.
Gather the pollen that they bring
for seeds to sprout new blooms next spring.

Flowers attract butterflies and bees,
which spread the pollen flowers need.
Then the flowers make fruit and seeds.
Oh, flowers, yes, they make seeds!

Flowers attract butterflies and bees,
which spread the pollen flowers need.
Then the flowers make fruit and seeds.
Oh, flowers, yes, they make seeds!

Fancy Flowers

Hip Hop
Drew Temperante

Intro

One, two, three, four, five, six! Six plant parts and they go like this: roots, stems, leaves, flow-ers, fruit, and seeds!

Each part plays a spe-cial role. Flow-ers help plants to grow and grow.

Chorus

Flow-ers at-tract but-ter-flies and bees, which spread the pol-len flow-ers need. Then the flow-ers make fruit and seeds. Oh,

flow-ers, yes, they make seeds!

Verse

1. Flow-ers, they make quite a show on a pond or a wind-y mead-ow. Farm-ers grow flow-ers they hope to sell in eve-ry col-or, shape, and smell.

Chorus

Verse 2
Eat some flowers. Have a bowl
of cauliflower casserole.
Butter artichokes and broccoli.
Sip a cup of chamomile tea!

Bridge

Eve-ry-one do the flow-er bal-let, sway-ing on a sum-mer's day. O-pen your pet-als. Shake them out, so bees can see what you're all a-bout. Fill the

air with a scent so sweet. But-ter-flies will flut-ter at your feet. Gath-er the pol-len that they bring for seeds to sprout new blooms next spring.

Chorus (x2)

GLOSSARY

artichokes—plants in the thistle family with large, prickly flowers that can be cooked and eaten

attract—to cause something to move closer or touch

cauliflower—a vegetable with a large, round white head

chamomile—a type of plant with flowers that can be dried and used to make tea

pollen—tiny yellow grains produced by flowers

scent—a smell, especially a pleasant one

GUIDED READING ACTIVITIES

1. This book has pictures of many flowers. Find one you like, and draw one of your own!

2. People often like to decorate with flowers. Do you have flowers in your house? What about in your classroom? Do you have any flowers in your room?

3. It's fun to give flowers to a friend or someone in your family. If you were buying flowers, what colors would you get? Who would you give them to?

TO LEARN MORE

Bishop, Celeste. *Why Do Plants Have Flowers?* New York: PowerKids Press, 2016.

Clay, Kathryn. *Flowers*. North Mankato, MN: Capstone, 2016.

Pendergast, George. *Flowers: From Seeds to Bloom*. New York: Gareth Stevens, 2016.

Throp, Claire. *All about Flowers*. Chicago: Capstone Heinemann Library, 2015.